KARATE KID

by Rosanne L. Kurstedt

Illustrated by Mark Chambers

RP|KIDS
PHILADELPHIA

Karate Kid, a student of Karate (*Karateka*), practices. He puts on his uniform (*gi*) and ties his belt (*obi*). He bows as he enters the Dojo. This is a sign of respect.

"*Kyotsuke*," Sensei calls.

Karate Kid stands at attention (*Masubi Dachi*).

He bows to the front—acknowledging the past masters (*Shomen ni Rei*).

He bows to his instructor—a signal of gratitude (*Sensei ni Rei*).

He bows to his classmates—a sign of support (*Otagai ni Rei*).

On the mat he stretches, breathes, and calms his thoughts (*Mokuso*).

(DACHI)

Ready Stance

(HACHIJI DACHI)

With feet shoulder-width apart, arms slightly forward, fists toward the floor, Karate Kid imagines moving nimbly into other stances.

Front Stance

(ZENKUTSU DACHI)

Karate Kid steps one foot forward then *slides* it out. His front knee bent and his back knee straight, Karate Kid inhales. Exhales. Connects.

Horse-Riding Stance

(KIBA DACHI)

Like sitting in a saddle, Karate Kid steps wide with both knees bent. Solid. Steady. Unshakeable.

Cat Stance

(NEKO ASHI DACHI)

Karate Kid sets one foot in front of the other lightly. Like a cat, with weight on his back foot, he bends his knees slightly. He's ready to pounce, swiftly.

KICKS

(GERI)

Front Kick

(MAE GERI)

From a front stance, Karate Kid lifts his back knee. Then he extends the leg, kicking forward. Like a snake's tongue, he snaps his leg out and in. Fast. Unexpected. Poised.

Side-Thrusting Kick

(YOKO GERI KEKOMI)

In one fluid motion, Karate Kid raises his knee, turns his hip, twists his foot, and snaps his leg forward. He strikes with intention. Balance. Speed.

Roundhouse Kick

(MAWASHI GERI)

Karate Kid lifts one leg with his foot as high as his knee. He prepares to strike high or low. His foot flicks forward then snaps back. He settles into his stance. Quick. Powerful. Calm.

Back Kick

(USHIRO GERI)

Karate Kid brings his back knee forward, rotating on his front leg. Turning. Twisting. Building power. Karate Kid *strikes* with the heel of his foot. Commanding. Confident. Forceful.

PUNCHES / STRIKES

(ZUKI) / (UCHI)

Stepping or Front Punch

(OI-ZUKI)

Step. Punch out. Step. Punch out. Karate Kid's fists turn and snap. Punctuated. Determined. Deliberate.

Back-Fist Strike

(URAKEN UCHI)

Karate Kid looks at the target and crosses his arms, elbows touching. His top elbow *whips* toward the target and the back knuckles *strike*, while the bottom arm *snaps* back to his hip. He's in position for the next move.

Spear-Hand Strike

(NUKITE)

Fingers are zipped, stiff, and rigid. Thumb is tucked. Karate Kid's hand pierces through the air. Versatile. Flexible. Direct.

Eagle-Hand Strike

(WASHI DE UCHI)

Karate Kid's fingers are pinched like
an eagle's beak as they peck and jab.
Pointed. Intense. Precise.

(UKEI)

Downward Block

(GEDAN BARAI UKE)

Karate Kid crosses his arms. He drives the top arm forward and down, blocking low. Then, he draws the other arm back, fist rotating into place. Energized. Centered. Fixed.

Rising Block

(AGE UKE)

Karate Kid's arm rotates and
snaps in front of his forehead.
Steady. Secure. Safe.

Inside Block

(UCHI UKE)

One arm straight. One arm bent. Karate
Kid pulls back and twists his wrist—quick.
Deflecting. Protecting.

Knife-Hand Block

(SHUTO UKE)

Karate Kid's hand slices through the air.
He blocks. Skilled. Sharp. Definitive.

Katas

Focused, Karate Kid uses all that he has learned. Power, speed, and flow. Like a dance, Karate Kid blocks and attacks imaginary opponents. "*Kiai*!"

Karate Kid returns to *Hachiji Dachi*, ready position. He breathes and thinks about the class. (*Mokuso*)

He bows to his classmates—a sign of support (*Otagai ni Rei*).

He bows to his instructor—a signal of gratitude (*Sensei ni Rei*).

He bows to the front—acknowledging the past masters (*Shomen ni Rei*).

Karate Kid is ready to face every challenge with confidence.

A Note for Parents

Karate comes from two Japanese words: *kara*, meaning "empty" or "open," and *te*, meaning "hand." *Karate Kid* focuses on the basics *(Kihon)* of karate, which includes:

Stances (Dachi): The foundation for strength and confidence.
Kicks (Geri): Flexibility, power, and balance are essential.
Punches (Zuki)/Strikes (Uchi): Using various parts of the hand or fist, punches and strikes require intensity and agility.
Blocks (Uke): By anticipating moves, blocks protect.

Karate Kid addresses another aspect of karate, too—the ***Katas***, which are sequences of movements put together, almost like a dance.

Originally developed as a form of self-defense, modern-day karate has evolved into a sport and a way of life that develops both mental and physical discipline. At the heart of karate is respect—for self, for the art, and for others. Students of karate learn techniques by practicing movements over and over. The repetitive practice requires concentration and self-control, which leads to improved focus.

Even young students of karate begin to recognize how deliberate practice helps them gain confidence, build strength, and move up belt levels. Because of karate's clear goals and expectations, students of karate come to understand that a positive attitude and perseverance can help them to overcome challenges in their daily lives with confidence.

Many thanks to Julie Matysik from Running Press Kids, Liza Fleissig and Ginger Harris from the Liza Royce Agency, Laura Sassi, one of my many writing friends who was particularly supportive of me through this project, and, as always, my family.

I'd like to also thank Arthur Hearns, Sensei,
owner of Hands of Life Martial Arts in New Jersey, for his guidance.

Running Press Kids
Hachette Book Group
1290 Avenue of the Americas, New York, NY 10104
www.runningpress.com/rpkids
@RP_Kids

Printed in China

First Edition: September 2019

Published by Running Press Kids, an imprint of Perseus Books, LLC, a subsidiary of Hachette Book Group, Inc. The Running Press Kids name and logo is a trademark of the Hachette Book Group.

Print book cover and interior design by Christopher Eads.

Library of Congress Control Number: 2018963236

ISBNs: 978-0-7624-9343-2 (hardcover), 978-0-7624-9342-5 (ebook),
978-0-7624-9344-9 (ebook), 978-0-7624-9345-6 (ebook)

1010

10 9 8 7 6 5 4 3 2 1